How Our Government Spending is Effecting Our Mentally Ill and Our Future

How Our Government Spending is Effecting Our Mentally Ill and Our Future

---

A PERSONAL VIEW

Dawn Todd, M.S.

Rev. date: 03/11/2016

CONTENTS

DEDICATION

This book is dedicated to all the individuals that have some form of mental defect and for their family/caregivers that have given up their lives to take care of these individuals. These individuals need more appropriate help and the only way that this can happen is if more monies are put into our mental health system and more research being completed. The children of today is our country's future, if we as a society do not make the government accountable for the budget cuts to our mental health system the budget cuts will continue and the help will become less available. With the right kind of help our high functioning mentally ill can become productive individuals in our communities. These individuals have the same feelings that everybody else has. The question to ask is: If your child had cancer would you want them to get the appropriate treatment or just be treated like second class citizens that would never have a chance to be a productive citizen? Just because individuals are different it does not give our government the right to discriminate.

ABSTRACT

There are several different ways that the American Government spends our tax payer's monies without us knowing about it. Some of this Government spending is ridiculous when looking at the bigger picture of what is actually going on in the United States. The mentally ill need more help and that can only be met by Community Mental Health (CMH) receiving more monies. If that was to happen there could be less false complaints to Child Protective Services (CPS) and also less monies put into the Criminal Justice System. There are several inmates in our prisons and jails that are mentally ill and not receiving the treatment that they need, which leads to more recidivism.

INTRODUCTION

I am an American Citizen; I was born in Flint, Michigan. I am now 48 years old and have been working since I have been 16. I now have a herniated disc, bulging disc. Scoliosis, degenerative disc disease, degenerative joint disease, I have had two Transient Ischemic Attacks (TIA), spondylosis, and severe recurrent major depression. I have applied for disability, because of the physical pain that I am in and am not able to do what I used to. Most of my working history has been in manufacturing.

I have completed schooling for a bachelor's degree in Criminal Justice and a Master's Degree in Forensic Psychology. However, after I received my Bachelor's Degree I wanted to work in a Crime Lab, but did not have experience so I was denied. Then I went on to receive my Master's in Forensic Psychology in research and planning through Walden University online. Through that program I did not receive a practicum or internship, because for research you are not supposed to have to be licensed. This was told to me by the State of Michigan. However, I have tried to find a job in research in psychology with no avail, because I am not licensed. I now have a student loan debt of about $138,000.00 with no aspect of finding a job.

I have been denied disability because I still have a thought process—never mind that my body does not work the way that it did and I have paid into the system for 32 years. Part of the reason for the herniated disc and the bulging disc is because we have a mentally challenged daughter who has dissociative identity disorder (DID) with cognitive impairment and homicidal and suicidal tendencies. One evening about a week before she turned 18 I had to restrain her (police hold) because she was out of control and that is when I received those injuries.

To sum it up. I paid into social security for 32 years, have had to fight Community Mental Health to get help for our daughter (which was and is seriously lacking), and because she really did not get the help that she needed I was injured. I also continued in my education to try to help with research for our mentally ill individuals. I believe that I have done everything that I possibly could and for what? To have my government turn their backs on me, an American Citizen, who helps pay their salary.

GOVERNMENT SPENDING

We hear about government spending and budget cuts all the time. Many individuals would like to know where their tax dollars are going. Do to my situation that was explained in the introduction, I did a little bit of research on the internet and have been to some meetings about cutting the mental health budget.

On the internet I found: "30 Stupid Thing The Government Is Spending Money On" (Snyder, M. February 29, 2012) and "Here's a List of Stupid Things the Government Spends Money Onw" (Knakal, R. October 1, 2013). The first 30 in this list is quoted from the first reference, the rest of the list is quoted from the second reference. The lists are:

1. The U.S. government is spending $750,000 on a new soccer field for detainees held at Guantanamo Bay.
2. The Obama administration plans to spend between 16 and 20 million dollars helping students from Indonesia get master's degrees.
3. If you can believe it, the U.S. government has spent $175,587 to determine if cocaine makes Japanese quail engage in sexually risky behavior.
4. The U.S. government spent $200,000 on a tattoo removal program in Mission Hills, California.

5. The federal government has shelled out $3million to researchers at the University of California at Irvine to fund their research on video games such as World of Warcraft.

6. The Department of Health and Human Services plans to spend $500 million on a program that will, among other things, seek to solve the problem of 5-year-old children that "can't sit still" in a kindergarten classroom.

7. Fannie Mae is about to ask the federal government for another $4.6 billion bailout and it will almost certainly get it.

8. The federal government once spent 30 million dollars on a program that was designed to help Pakistani farmers produce more mangos.

9. The U.S. Department of Agriculture once gave researchers at the University of New Hampshire $700,000 to study methane gas emissions from dairy cows.

10. According to USA Today, 13 different government agencies "fund 209 different science, technology, engineering and math (STEM) education programs—and 173 of those programs overlap with at least one other program."

11. A total of $615,000 was given to the University of California at Santa Cruz to digitize photos, T-shirts and concert tickets belonging to the Grateful Dead.

12. China lends us more money than any other foreign nation, but that didn't stop our government

from spending 17.8 million dollars on social and environmental programs for China.

13. The U.S. government once spent 2.6 million dollars to train Chinese prostitutes to drink responsibly.

14. One professor at Stanford University was given $239,100 to study how the Americans use the internet to find love.

15. The U.S. Postal Service spent $13,500 on a single dinner at Ruth's Chris Steakhouse.

16. The National Science Foundation once spent $216,000 to study whether or not politicians "gain or lose support by taking ambiguous positions".

17. A total of $1.8 million was spent on a "museum of neon signs" in Las Vegas, Nevada.

18. The federal government spends 25 billion dollars a year maintaining federal buildings that are either unused or totally vacant.

19. U.S. farmers are given a total of $2 billion each year for not farming their land.

20. The U.S. government handed one Tennessee library $5,000 for the purpose of hosting a serious of video game parties.

21. A few years ago the government spent $123,050 on a Mother's Day Shrine in Grafton, West Virginia. It turns out the Grafton only has a population of a little more than 5,000 people.

22. One professor at Dartmouth University was given $137,530 to create a "recession-themed" video game entitled "Layoff".

23. According to the Heritage Foundation, the U.S. military spent "$998,798 shipping two 19-cent washers from South Carolina to Texas and $293,451 sending an 89-cent washer from South Carolina to Florida".

24. The U.S. Department of Agriculture once shelled out $30,000 to a group of farmers to develop a tourist-friendly database of farms that host guests for overnight "haycations".

25. The National Institutes of Health paid researchers $400,000 to find out why gay men in Argentina engage in risky sexual behavior when they are drunk.

26. The National Institutes of Health also spent $442,340 to study the behavior of male prostitutes in Vietnam.

27. The National Institutes of Health loves to spend our tax money on really bizarre things. The NIH once spent $800,000 in "stimulus funds" to study the impact of a "genital-washing program" on men in South Africa.

28. According to the Washington Post, 1,271 different government organizations work on government programs related to counterterrorism and homeland security.

29. The U.S. government spent $100,000 on a "Celebrity Chef Fruit Promotion Road Show in Indonesia".

30. The feds once gave Alaska Airlines $500,000 "to paint a Chinook salmon" on the side of a Boeing 737.

31. The government spends about $100 million every four years to subsidize parties at the political conventions.

32. The Department of Agriculture spent $2 million to fund an internship program. The program hired one full-time intern.

33. In 2012, $120 million was paid to dead federal employees.

34. A total of $146 million was paid for federal employees to upgrade their flights to business class.

35. The Department of Health and Human Services provided an $800,000 subsidy to build IHop in Washington, D.C.

36. The National Institutes of Health has given $1.5 million to Brigham and Women's Hospital in Boston to study why "three-quarters" of lesbians in the United States are overweight and why most gay males are not.

37. During 2012, $25,000 of federal money was spent on a promotional tour for the Alabama Watermelon Queen.

38. The U.S. government spent $505,000 "to promote specialty hair and beauty products for cats and dogs" in 2012.

39. NASA spends close to $1 million per year developing a menu of food for a manned mission to Mars even though it is being projected that a manned mission to Mars is still decades away.

40. Over the past 15 years, a total of approximately $5.25 million has been spent on hair care services for the U.S. Senate.

41. The U.S. government spent $27 million to teach Moroccans how to design and make pottery in 2012.

42. During fiscal year 2012, the National Science Foundation gave researchers at Purdue University $350,000. They used part of that money to help fund a study that discovered that if golfers imagine that a hole is bigger it will help them with their putting.

43. A total of $10,000 of U.S. taxpayer money was actually used to purchase talking urinal cakes in Michigan.

44. Vice President Joe Biden and his staff stopped in Paris for one night in February 2013. The hotel bill for that one night came to $585,000.

45. The U.S. Department of Agriculture has spent $300,000 to encourage Americans to eat caviar produced in Idaho.

46. The National Institute of Health recently gave $666,905 to a group of researchers that is conducting a study on the benefits of watching reruns on television.

47. The National Institute of Health also spent $592,527 on a study that sought to figure out once and for all why chimpanzees throw poop.

48. The IRS spent $60,000 on a film parody of Star Trek and a film parody of Gilligan's Island.

49. In 2012, the government spent just under $1 million posting snippets of poetry in zoos around the country.

50. The U.S. Air Force Office of Scientific Research spent $300,000 on a study that concluded the first bird on earth probably had black feathers.

51. The federal government spent $75,000 to promote awareness about the role Michigan plays in producing Christmas trees and poinsettias.

Now all this money adds up to $30,592,558,788 that could be spent on more important issues facing America and this list is just a small example. One of the issues that some of this money could be utilized on wisely would be more research on mental health issues. If some of this money was spent on more research in the mental health issues facing America today maybe our prisons would not be so full. I do not know about the rest of the Americans, but I feel that the U.S. government needs to help the true Americans before others. If the foundation (America) falls apart what would happen?

I do not know how the rest of the American citizens feel about this foolish spending, but I am not happy with it at all. For instance instead of paying $750,000 for a new soccer field in Guantanamo Bay why not put that money in our children's schools (the American future). Instead of spending between 16 and 20 million dollars for helping students of Indonesia receive their Master's Degree why not help the struggling Americans receive their education. An example of this is that I am tapped out on my Financial Aid and only need $40,000 to finish my PhD in Forensic psychology to be able to help people. My tax money is going to pay for an Indonesian's schooling when I cannot even afford my own education. Something is wrong with that picture. Who cares about Japanese Quails sexual behavior? Seeking to solve the problem of why 5 year olds not sitting still in a kindergarten classroom could be beneficial, but part of the reason is because children do not play outside as much as I did when I was a kid. Instead they are playing video games or on a computer. How are they supposed to dispense their energy when there is no physical release of their energy? I could go on and on in disputing just about everything on this list, but I think you get the picture.

I do know that there is always some type of research going on for the mental health, but I also know that there are a lot of gaps in the research. I do have a couple of ideas that could possibly close a couple of gaps. However, because I cannot take the test to become a licensed forensic psychologist because the program that I completed did not require a practicum, I cannot find a job doing this research. Now I have reached the maximum of financial aid I cannot go for a PhD in Forensic Psychology, but our government is willing to pay 16 to 20 million dollars for individuals from Indonesia get master's degrees. I only need $40,000 to go for my PhD. Why cannot our government help me with the $40,000 so that I can help individuals that are mentally ill and possibly reduce the prison population in America?

To me America needs to take care of Americans first. I do believe in helping other people, but we need to take care of own first. I have seen so many families struggling with some form of mental issues in their family and not receiving the proper help. This is why I would like to pursue a PhD in Forensic Psychology; so that I can complete research and help on planning new treatments, so that these families and individuals can receive the help that they need.

MENTAL HEALTH ISSUES IN THE U.S.

S ince the starting of the closures of the Mental Health
Institutes (deinstitutionalization) there has been a
spike in the number of mentally ill inmates in the U.S.
prisons and jails. The prisons and jails in America have
become the holding tanks for our mentally ill. "In 2012,
there were an estimated 356,268 inmates with severe
mental illnesses in U.S. prisons and jails. There were
only 35,000 mentally ill individuals in state psychiatric
hospitals" (Lewis, R. p2 April 8, 2014).

The money that has been spent on the list above
among other things could have been better spent on more
research on our mentally ill individuals. The reasons for the
deinstitutionalization was to let the mentally ill live in the
least restrictive environment and let the community handle
the treatment of the mentally ill. However, the mentally
ill population was more than what the community could
handle (Mental Health and the Role of the States, 2015).
There are not enough mental health workers available
in the community to help the number of our mentally ill
individuals. With the workers that are available they have
too many clients to be able to give intensive therapy to

the clients that need it. I know this through my personal experience that will be explained in detail in a later chapter.

The reason why more research and treatment planning is important in today's society is because of the number of inmates that are mentally ill and not receiving the appropriate treatment. "There are 10 times more mentally ill Americans in prisons and jails than in state psychiatric hospitals" (Lewis, R. p1 April 8, 2014). In today's society there is not a valid reason for the way that our mentally ill inmates are treated, often times these mentally ill individuals are worse when they are released back into society (Lewis, R. April 8, 2014). There will be a later chapter that goes more in depth of what our mentally ill inmates go through in our prisons and jails.

Budget cuts for treatment of our mentally ill have actually increased our debt in the United States. It costs more for a mentally ill inmate than what it would cost for them to receive the proper treatment. Another way that the lack of proper treatment for our mentally ill has affected our economy is loss of work, not only for the mentally ill individual but also for family members/caretakers of the mentally ill individuals. I know that I would receive several calls when I was working and I had to rush home to either calm my daughter down or call the police to take her into the emergency room, where at times we would have to wait there the whole weekend for a bed to become open in a mental hospital. I believe that the longest wait was 72 hours. Then when they finally do get into a mental hospital the stay is anywhere from 3 to 10 days. This is just a band aid and in my experience it does not take long until it is another trip to the emergency room.

One of the biggest gaps that I have seen in all of my literature reviews on any type of mental illness is how cognitive impairment plays a role in the treatment plan. I have been told several times by therapists/counselors that a treatment plan for cognitive impairment does not exist. This is one place that there needs to be some kind of research completed. When looking for treatment of cognitive impairments on the internet it brought me to articles about aging, dementia, Alzheimer, and brain injuries. What about individuals that are born with cognitive impairment? These individuals often are born with some other type of mental issue that goes along with cognitive impairment, but until the cognitive impairment can be treated how can treatment for the other mental issue be effective?

Cognitive impairment is placed on a scale of mild to profound going by the individuals IQ. I personally know a person that has a normal IQ, but has some cognitive impairment. With some individuals it is hard to tell if they have a cognitive impairment, because they can tell you right from wrong and they can also tell you some consequences of their actions, but that does not stop them from doing something wrong or dangerous. An example of this is my daughter; she is classified as being mildly cognitively impaired. You can ask her if she should go with strangers and her answer would be no and she can also tell you what could happen to her if she did go with a stranger (e.g. raped or killed). Now if you were to ask her if she would still go with a stranger that had a baby, puppy, kitten, or candy, she would tell you that yes she would go. When a mental health professional asks individuals if they know right from wrong and what the consequences could be and these individuals know the correct answers the mental health professional does not go further and ask if the individual would still go through with whatever action they are asking about.

Some aspects of life that can be affected by cognitive impairment could be within the legal system (which there will be more detail in a later chapter), in the working environment, and in society in general. Cognitive impairment can affect individuals in different ways and different aspects of their life. Whatever the case may be of how the individual's life is affected by cognitive impairment, there needs to be more research completed on how to help these individuals so that they can live a more productive life. In my opinion this is one of the places that need to be one of the top conditions that need to be researched. Without treatment for cognitive impairment how can the individuals truly understand their treatment plan? This is one example that I feel a portion of the tax payer's monies should go. It could possibly help some high functioning mentally ill individuals become more productive, which in turn could help the U.S. economy.

Cognitive impairment can be associated with Fetal Alcohol Spectrum Disorder (FASD). The term FASD is an umbrella term for alcohol related birth defects, which include Fetal Alcohol Syndrome (FAS), Partial Fetal Alcohol Syndrome (pFAS), Alcohol-Related Neurodevelopment Disorder (ARND), Static Encephalopathy/Alcohol Exposed (SE/AE), and Neurobehavioral Disorder/Alcohol Exposed

(ND/AE) (Substance Abuse and Mental Health Services Administration 2014). It is estimated that 1 to 3 per 1,000 live births will be affected by FASD, but in high risk population that number grows to 10 to 15 per 1,000 live births. (Adubato, S., & Cohen, D., 2011). Many individuals that fall within the FASD umbrella do not function as well as what you would think they would going by their IQ, they are slower in reaching their milestones and are often very naïve and gullible (Kellerman, T. (n.d.). "Other disorders that may occur along with FASD include: Attention Deficit Disorder (ADD/ADHD), Depression, Reactive Attachment Disorder (RAD), Bipolar Disorder, Obsessive Compulsive Disorder (OCD), Pervasive Development Disorder (PDD), Asperger Syndrome (mild Autism), Tourette Syndrome, Mental Retardation, or Developmental Delays (Kellerman, T. (n.d.). Several individuals that fall within the FASD umbrella end up dropping out of school, find themselves in trouble with the law, do not act appropriately socially, have inappropriate sexual behaviors, have addictive personalities, are often depressed, and have suicidal tendencies (Kellerman, T. (n.d.).

In my opinion I would rather see the $1.8 million that was spent on a "museum of neon signs" in Las Vegas, Nevada go to more research on how to help these individuals that fall under the FASD umbrella and to also help teachers learn how to teach these children and for law enforcement personnel to understand FASD better. I do believe that this would be a better way for the U.S. Government to spend our tax dollars. When it comes to students that fall within the FASD umbrella our public school system does not know how to handle the situation. I was involved with an Individualized Educational Placement (IEP) with a student that has FAS. To me this IEP was a joke. The student was mainstreamed with some special accommodations. The accommodations were for the student to tell the teacher if he was going to need more time to complete the assignment when the assignment was handed out, now if that assignment was a 10 page essay that was due in 3 weeks how would the student know if he would need more time at the time the assignment was given. This student does not know what his assignments in his other classes are going to be within the next three weeks. Also, in his IEP it was listed that he could have more time to take a test/quiz and could be placed in the hallway or another room for less distraction. One teacher of this student did not understand what this meant. This is where money could be spent on educating teachers on how and what accommodations need to be made for students that fall under the FASD umbrella.

As for the law enforcement personnel, they need to be educated on everything that has to do with FASD and any mental health issue. The lack of knowledge on the law enforcement system has let our FASD and mentally ill go through a lot of needless suffering and in some instances has even caused death. Through many of the literature reviews that I have had to do for my schooling there is one thing that I read that sticks in my mind it is: The judicial system was built for consequences not for treatment. Which is true, however with all the budget cuts to the mental health system and so many of our mentally ill citizens ending up in the criminal justice system it is time to take another look at what is going on. Either stop the budget cuts to the mental health system and give them more money to provide the beds that are needed or make special sections in all the jails and prisons so that our mentally ill can get the treatment that they deserve and need. These individuals did not ask to be born like this or to have an injury that caused their condition, but our government is treating them like second class citizens. Does the U.S. Government treat someone with cancer as a second class citizen? The individuals that fall under the FASD umbrella or are classified as mentally ill have a disease and our government is punishing them for having that disease instead of helping them.

Autism effects all walks of life the recent diagnosis of Autism of a prominent politician family member was instrumental in the resurgence of Autism research. However, there still needs to be more research completed and the treatment needs to be more readily available. The proper treatment for any form of mental health is only available to the families that have money. In many states our government officials tell the parents of the child that has a mental illness to get them in a mental hospital and do not pick them up when they are released. Although the parents will have to take an abandonment rap, their mentally ill child will get better treatment. I would really like someone to explain to me how that really helps the family. To me that would do more damage to the mentally ill child, because that could cause abandonment issues itself. I know that my daughter would be devastated if we did that to her. However, in the state of Michigan that is not an option, because they have no place to place these mentally ill individuals. Which the $17.8 million that our government spent on social and environmental programs for China could help to make programs for our mentally ill more assessable and possibly even more available beds.

There are some places that provide some overnight care (called Respite) for a mentally ill child, how many nights depends on the organization that you are with and how much money the organization has to put into that fund. Being a parent of a mentally ill child I know Respite has helped us out when our daughter was not bad enough to go into the hospital but to out of control to stay home. Thanks to the budget cuts to mental health the respite home that we utilized when our daughter still lived with us may be closing its doors December 31, 2015. With having a mentally ill child there are several individuals that do not want your child to spend the night, because they are afraid of what the child may do and they do not know how to handle a situation that might come up. With our daughter every sharp object had to be locked up and we had to listen to see if she would get up in the middle of the night and get into something that she was not supposed to, I have spent several nights staying up all night because our daughter was not having a good night. So, I cannot blame other individuals for not wanting her to spend the night. Every time my daughter ask if she could spend the night somewhere we would always make up some kind of excuse so that the other individual would not feel bad telling her no.

In order for Community Mental Health to be less strict on the criteria for admission to mental hospitals they need more funding for more beds. "The federal government spends 25 billion dollars a year maintaining federal buildings that are either unused or totally vacant" (Snyder, M. February 29, 2012). Instead of having these buildings vacant why cannot the federal government put some money into turning these buildings into long term mental hospitals? I am not talking about keeping an individual in there for a lifetime, but something like from 6 months to 2 years depending on the severity of the individual and giving them the proper treatment. A better use of tax payers monies than paying $120 million to dead federal employees.

COMMUNITY MENTAL HEALTH

There are several different aspects of Community Mental Health (CMH). Here in Oakland county Michigan there is Macomb Oakland Regional Center (MORC), Easter Seals, Oakland Family Services, and Common Ground. Common Ground is the place that determines if the individual is going to be hospitalized. The main criteria for hospitalization are: "Is the person at harm to themselves or others?" If the individual is lucky enough to be admitted to a hospital it is only for a short-term (3 to 10 days) hospitalization, then it is up to the psychiatrist at the hospital if they need to be transferred to a long-term facility (usually 3 to 4 weeks). We only have two long term hospitals in the state of Michigan and both are very difficult to get into. If you do not have an organization (MORC, Easter Seals, or Oakland Family Services) that you are working with at this point they give you one. The first time that we took our daughter in they set us up with MORC. How they determine which organization to use goes by whether your child is classified as Developmentally Delayed (DD) or Cognitively Impaired (CI). Our daughter is both DD and CI; however, they classified her as DD. Having a classification of DD we could either work with MORC or Easter Seals. We ended up with MORC, which actually turned out to be the right organization because of one of her diagnosis is

Dissociative Identity Disorder (DID), which is the new name for Multiple Personalities and Easter Seals does not accept patients that have DID. Also MORC has more placement availability for Semi Independent Placement (SIP) homes and group homes. However, MORC's therapists/counselors, psychologists, and psychiatrists need smaller caseloads so that they can give more intensive treatment.

Now let's talk about how Obamacare has affected the mental health care system. The webpage http://obamacarefacts.com/obamacare-pros-and-cons/states that "Due to the sheer volume of the reforms, some of them, while well-intended, will inevitably have unintended consequences that warrant adjustments". According to a meeting that I went to about the Lahser Respite Home possibly having to close their doors, one of the unintended consequences from Obamacare is that because Medicaid has covered more individuals so they had to re-appropriate some monies. Some of the monies that were re-appropriated were monies for respite care. As a parent of a child that has mental problems the Lahser Respite Home was a savior to us. It is not easy to take care of a mentally challenged child 24/7, it was nice to be able to take our daughter to a home that would keep her overnight or possibly the whole weekend just to give us a break, and every parent needs a break once in a while. Even though our daughter is now in a SIP home and we do not need to utilize the Lahser Respite Home anymore, I know that there are many other families that could benefit from the break that they provide for the parents.

If respite is cut to the point that it is not available to provide relieve for the parents of the mentally challenged children the police and Children Protective Services (CPS) will become more involved. I cannot begin to tell you how many times I have had to call the police on my own daughter because she was so out of control that someone would have been hurt. There were also a number of times that our daughter lied about something that brought CPS into our lives. These are a couple of the reasons why more money needs to go toward mental health services instead of being cut from the mental health services. Instead of spending 30 million dollars for a program to help Pakistani farmers how to produce more mangos maybe that 30 million dollars should have been spent on training our law enforcement officers and our CPS workers how to deal with individuals that are mentally ill. I would hope that they do already have some form of training, but from a parent of a mentally ill individual more training for our government officials need to be mandatory.

Let me share with you part of what I have learned by dealing with the mental health system for 17 years. The first three years dealing with the mental health system was in Florida and the other 14 years has been in Michigan, which we are still dealing with. Getting the doctors to listen to the parents is very difficult. In Florida the doctors and the school told us that our daughter would not be able to learn so they just wanted to socialize her. In Michigan we had one forensic psychologist that did actually listen to us and he came up with the correct diagnosis, which was DID. However, because DID is such a controversial diagnosis MORC and other psychiatrists would not go along with the diagnosis until she turned 18. The books that are utilized in colleges and universities do not go into DID that much, which I think they should. How many other individuals are going through life with the wrong diagnosis just because it is controversial? This is another area of research that needs more monies, maybe than it would not be so controversial and individuals could be correctly diagnosed. But to our American Government it is more important to spend "$400,000 to find out why gay men in Argentina engage in risky sexual behavior when they are drunk" (Snyder, M. February 29, 2012).

Our mental health system needs a complete overhaul. We have had so many issues with CMH and I have utilized the correct channels of going through recipient rights, which to no surprise the complaints were all unfounded except for one, but nothing was done about it. However, there was one complaint that we did put in and we heard nothing back from recipient rights, but the hospital did close down and opened back up under a new name. According to the state of Michigan; "Community Mental Health does not have to answer to anyone but the constituents of the county that they are located in". To me that just does not make sense there should be someone higher up in Lansing, Michigan that can hold them accountable. I have paid my taxes to pay their salaries but my daughter and several other individuals cannot get the help that they need, because the tax payers monies are going to pay for other things that have nothing to do with the United States or helping the U.S. citizens. For example; "The U.S. Air Force Office of Scientific Research spent $300,000 on a study that concluded the first bird on earth probably had black feathers" (Knakal, R. October 1, 2013).

Another issue that is very important to our mentally ill individuals is our education system. Our education system needs to be trained on how to handle individuals that are mentally ill and individuals that fall under the umbrella of FASD that often fall through the cracks. The individuals that fall under the umbrella of FASD often drop out of school because they have a harder time remembering assignments and when they are due. They often times have difficulty with higher functioning capabilities.

EDUCATIONAL SYSTEM

The top three sources for our educational system in 2014 were sales and use taxes, personal income tax, and property taxes (State Budget Office). However, there were a total of 8 educational funding resources for the educational system in the United States and they are: 1) Sales and use taxes (44.1%), 2) Income Tax (17.4%), 3) Property Tax (13.5%), 4) Federal Reserve (12.1%), 5) Miscellaneous Taxes (6.1%), 6) State Lottery Funds (5.6%), 7) General Fund (1.1%), and 8) Other (.2%) which total $13.4 billion (State Budget Office). I do not know about the other schools in Michigan, but in our school system we have outdated books and students cannot take books home to study without the parent signing the book out. I realize that the internet is utilized a lot for school projects, but what about families that cannot afford a computer or the internet. Also, what about children learning how to spell? We had another daughter that was in a learning disability class, which is basically a slow learner. She had problems spelling and at her Individualized Education Placement (IEP) we asked about her lack of ability to spell and the answer that we were given was that there was spell check so they really were not worried about her lack of being able to spell. Which could explain why the U.S. ranks 2nd in ignorance (Ranking America).

When I was in school we had books that we used in school and we took those same books home to do homework and study. We also had sports teams that we had to compete to get on, but did not have to pay to play. With today's economy it is difficult to for some parents to pay for their child to try to get on a team and if their child does not make the team the parents are out of the money. I can understand teaching our children how to use the internet and the new technology, but what happens when our children need to go back to doing research the old fashioned way? In the school district that we are in my daughter's friend taught her about porn sights and she got in trouble for going there, which her punishment was to not be able to go on the computer for a month, which we did not have a problem with. But nothing happened to her friend that showed her where to go, which we do not think was fair. Also, the children can get on Facebook while on the school's computer. Would someone like to explain to me how that is educational? I do not feel that going on Facebook on the school's computer is appropriate or educational and I also feel that the school needs better filters for porn sites.

Now let's talk about IEP's. The school in Florida tested my youngest daughter, the one with the mental problems and came up with an IQ of 71, which is right above mental retardation, but told us that they only wanted to socialize her because she would not be able to learn. That did not sound right to us so we asked for a meeting with the individual that tested her and this individual came right out and told us that he prompted her more than what he should have to save the school some money. Here in Michigan the schools have to do their own testing instead of accepting testing from qualified individuals, which not only takes away from the time that these individuals could actually see someone to help them with an issue in school, but also is a waste of tax payer's monies. Most of these children do see a therapist/counselor and a psychiatrist outside of school. There are certain policies and rules that schools must abide by and some of these are found within the individuals with disabilities education act (IDEA). Why cannot the school take the testing that these individuals provide? Instead our federal government would rather spend $3 million to fund a research project on video games such as World of Warcraft (Snyder, M. February 29, 2012).

The director of special education in any school system is taught to save as much money as possible when it comes to tools to help the students. Several of the students that are in special education have social skills issues and there are a few of these students that need a one on one paraprofessional (teacher's helper). However, it is very difficult to receive a one on one paraprofessional, because it costs too much. Our government thinks that it is more important to spend $1.5 million to study why three-quarters of lesbians in the United States are overweight and why most gay males are not (Knakal, R. October 1, 2013). Where are our government's priorities? It is my opinion that more money needs to be spent on our children that are in school whether they are special needs or not, because they are our future. Students in the United States are near the middle of the pack compared to other countries. "The United States has one of the biggest gaps between high and low-performing students in an industrialized nation" (Wilde M. n.d.). This goes back to the need to put more financing in our special education classes.

Then there are children that are in between main stream and special education that are basically ignored and fall through the cracks. Some of these children fall under the FASD umbrella. Some of these individuals have an average IQ, but have cognitive/social issues. In several of these cases the individual is also diagnosed with bi-polar and ADHD, which is by itself problematic. This is one area that our schools need to help these individuals instead of punishing them; these individuals have a disorder that is not their fault. However, these children are often treated as difficult individuals who do not follow rules and try to push the limits. That is part of their disorder that the school personal does not know or do not want to face. Instead of spending money to complete research to help these students our government would rather spend money "$442,340 to study the behavior of male prostitutes in Vietnam" (Snyder, M. February 29, 2012). These types of individuals do better in smaller class sizes where there are less distractions and more individualized attention, but they do not fit in the typical special education classes.

One of the most important things to do when getting ready for an IEP is to have a copy of the section(s) of IDEA that pertain to your child's situation. The schools in Michigan will try anything not to have to spend the extra monies for these children. Some children are entitled to special transportation, but the school really wants to fight hard on that subject. One example of this is when our youngest child was in elementary they wanted her to walk to the bus stop at the office of the trailer park that we lived in, never mind that there was a street between us and the bus stop so we could not watch her. She should have been entitled to be picked up and dropped off at our home. Some of our children get bullied in school and even though there is a law against bullying, the school does nothing about the bullying. I have not only witnessed this with my own child, but I have also witnessed this with a couple of my nephew's. I had even printed out the law and taken up to the principal of the school and still nothing was done. So, now all of these children are going to different schools, even though our tax dollars are going to support the school in our district that did not support or defend our children. What kind of message is that sending?

When attending an IEP it is very important to understand the policies and laws or the school will get away with anything that they can. It is also a good idea to have either an advocate or a therapist/counselor or both attend these IEP meetings, because the schools are taught to save money anyway they can even it means not giving a child a service that they need. I have been to too many of these IEP meetings to know that the school will try to get out of anything that they possibly can and if the parent/guardian does not agree there is a box that they check stating that they do not agree with this IEP and they want a hearing. As a parent/guardian to a special needs child do not be afraid to check that box, if we do not advocate for our children who is going to? If the child feels that no one is fighting for them then why should they do their best and follow the policies when the school does not follow their own policies about bullying. At one point that child is going to take things into their own hands and either fight back and end up in jail or a mental hospital or the worst possible outcome is committing suicide.

CHILDREN PROTECTIVE SERVICES

Children Protective Services (CPS) was formed to help protect children and take them out of abusive situations, which is great when the child is actually being abused. However, today CPS has taken it to the extreme. A therapist has told me that according to CPS we are not allowed to spank our children. According to Michigan Abuse and Neglect Defense attorneys "Spanking, in and of itself, is not considered child abuse" (K & C Michigan Abuse and Neglect n.d.). However, when spanking a child the spanking cannot be in the extreme. "Michigan law defines child abuse as, harm or threatening harm to a child's health or welfare that occurs through non-accidental physical or mental injury, sexual abuse, sexual exploitation, or maltreatment" MCL § 722.622 (K & C Michigan Abuse and Neglect n.d.). I agree that there are some parents/caregivers that take spanking to the extreme and in those cases it should be classified as abuse, but I have also seen instances where a child should have been spanked and the child threatens the parents with CPS. It has come to the point that parents are afraid of spanking their child and in turn these children grow up thinking that they can do whatever they want to do and their parents cannot do anything about it, especially children that have a mental condition. Some individuals believe that spanking a child can lead to more aggressive behavior, low self-esteem, and drug use (Mince-Didier, A. n.d.). Has anyone wondered why there are more children getting into legal problems these days compared to when I was a child? When I was a child if we did something wrong we were spanked and if we did something wrong in school the teacher used a paddle on us. We were also more respectful of other individuals (especially the elderly) and had more respect for other individual's property. Individuals that are for spanking believe that spankings are an effective way of disciplining a child. However, spanking should be used when appropriate not for everything that the child does wrong (Mince-Didier, A. n.d.). An example of when I believe that spanking should be utilized is when a child attempts to be physically/verbally abusive toward a parent/ guardian. An example of when a spanking should not occur is when the child does not get off the computer/game console when told to do so, I feel that the appropriate punishment for something like that would be taking the computer/game console away for a couple days. Parents need to use common sense when utilizing spanking as a punishment.

CPS and therapist/counselors wants parents to use gentle teaching and time outs to discipline our children. My question to these professionals is have they ever raised a mentally challenged child and if they did how well did gentle teaching and time outs work for them? I have personally raised a mentally challenged child and have helped in the raising of other children that have mental issues and the gentle teaching or time outs did not work. When trying the gentle teaching or time outs some of these mentally challenged children yell, scream, throw things at you, or cuss at you and calling you all kinds of nasty names. CPS expects us as parents to take this abuse from our children. I would take things away from my daughter or make her sit in her room or send her outside until she cooled down so that we could talk about the problem. However, I cannot tell you how often my daughter went to school and exaggerated the truth, which in turn caused CPS to come into our lives. It seems to me that when CPS receives a phone call about a child being abused and they have had several calls about this child and every situation had been unfounded and they know the family and that the child has a mental problem, it would much cheaper to just make a phone call. The saving of money in this situation could free up some money for more research or more beds for the mentally ill. I cannot even tell you the amount of times that CPS has been in our lives and everything was unfounded. The last time that they were in our lives I became so depressed that I was diagnosed with severe major depression. At that time I was just ready to give up and tell CPS to take our daughter, because I was just so tired and beaten down by trying to get my daughter the proper help that she needed through CMH. My therapist was ready to put me in the hospital, but yet I was the one being accused of abusing my child.

CPS, DHS, and Family Independence Agency (FIA) (hereafter will be referred to as government agencies) are supposed to reunite the families if possible. However, these government agencies make the parents jump through so many hoops here in Michigan that it is nearly impossible especially for a single parent. The reason why the government agencies do this is because the state can make money if families are not reunited and the child is adopted. I have previously discussed the spanking laws in Michigan, now I will quote the FIA present state of law in the state of Michigan: "1) Parent cannot spank their child. Spanking, even with clothes covering the bottom, is severe physical abuse. Parents are only to use time out, reasoning and loss of privileges. 2) Parents cannot engage in physical self defense to protect themselves from a physically hostile teenager. An act of self defense by a parent is severe physical and emotional abuse. Parents are to use reasoning, time out and loss of privileges only and must sacrifice their safety for their violent teenager's safety. 3) Parents cannot argue or talk about adult subjects, such as family finances, in front of their children. These are subjects that the child has no control over and creates extreme emotional distress in the child. FIA has classified this area as emotional or environmental abuse and/or neglect of the child. 4) Parents with low income are neglecting their children's basic needs. Low income parents cannot provide for the proper medical, physical or emotional needs of their children due to their limited income. The parent's failure to obtain middle income jobs means environmental, medical and emotional neglect. 5) Parents that fail to take their child to the family physician for colds, flu, sniffles and mild congestion, or parents who fail to obtain a family pediatrician are neglecting the medical needs of their children. FIA has classified this as medical neglect. 6) Parents who own pornographic materials, such as magazines, books, video tapes, and conceal such materials from their children have created environmental and emotional neglect of their children. Parents who own and hide such material run the risk that children will find these materials and view them are causing emotional harm to their children. FIA has classified this as environmental neglect. 7) Divorced, single parent families seem to be targeted by FIA as high risk environments for emotional and environmental neglect. Most single parent families are low income and of course, according to FIA, cannot provide for the basic needs of the children as measured against income standards" (Frederick, J.M., October 24, 1999).

I once had a family member tell me that the Michigan government removes children from homes when they should not remove the children. This family member told me that Michigan does this to make money through adopting these children out to other families. I did not want to believe that, so I did some checking on these accusations and found out that this is true. The Michigan government agencies make it almost impossible for a single parent to get their child/ children back. These single parents need to make a living working outside of the home, which is held against them calling it "causing environmental and emotional neglect of the child" (Frederick, J.M., October 24, 1999).

The Michigan governmental agencies say that because the single parent is working outside of the home to make money to keep a roof over their children's heads, food on the table, and clothes on their back, the single parent is neglecting their child/children. What a catch 22? What I find interesting is that the Michigan government agencies utilize Friend of Court records and send what is supposed to be a prevention worker to the home of a single parent and offers the single parent different classes to help them. Now if the single parent follows up on these classes they are doing what the government agencies are suggesting, trying to keep them happy so that their children are not removed, which in turn takes the single parent out of the home more and the government agencies can use that against them because they are not home and they are neglecting their child/children. Most of the cases that FIA are involved in have come from families receiving voluntary services from these Michigan government agencies, not from schools or doctors that suspect child abuse (Frederick, J.M., October 24, 1999).

The reason why these families are targeted by the Michigan government agencies is to justify Michigan's need for State and Federal grants, so individuals can keep their jobs. For each child that is placed in foster care FIA receives $2,000 to $4,000 a month from Federal grants and $10,000 for each child that is adopted and the state of Michigan matches these funds. For each child that a social worker takes out of a home that leads to an adoption the social worker receives a bonus (Frederick, J.M., October 24, 1999). I believe that the social worker should receive a bonus for reuniting a family, not tearing a family apart, with the bonuses that they have in place now it's no wonder way there is not enough foster homes. To me this is a disgrace to the state of Michigan and to the United States for letting this happen.

Another reason that these government agencies find to remove the child from the home is because the parent(s) do not take their child/children to the doctor because they have the sniffles. However, living in Michigan just about every child is going to catch a cold or have sniffles just because of the weather. Most of the time the doctors do not give out any prescriptions and just prescribe over the counter medication, which in turn cost more money either to the parents or the state (if the child is on Medicaid). Now if the child is really sick and had been sick for more than a few days and the parents do not do anything then I could understand the state stepping in.

However, most of these situations end up with legal litigations. Which again in most cases is a waste of tax payer's monies? Parents need to be able to raise their children without the government agencies stepping in unless necessary. When I was growing up if children did something that was wrong they received a spanking and my generation grew up with more respect for elders and authority figures. In today's world the children and teenagers have a lot less respect for anything or anybody, which causes more legal problems. So with the gentle teaching method are we really helping our child/children or are we setting them up for failure, because the legal system is charging younger children as adults with adult consequences.

JUSTICE SYSTEM

The American Justice system does not know how to handle individuals with a mental illness or a FASD. There needs to be more training for the individuals in the justice system such as: judges, prosecuting attorneys, probation officers, and correctional officers. Especially since our mentally ill end up in our jails and prisons and do not receive the help that they desperately need. Since our government started shutting down the asylums and letting the community take care of our mentally ill and the government has cut billions of dollars from mental health our mentally ill are basically ending up in the same situation that they were in while they were in the asylums: locked up behind bars (Sullivan, L., January 20, 2014).

Tom Dart is the sheriff in Cook County, Ill. The jail there is basically like a small city, however there are about a third of these inmates that have some kind of mental defect. Sheriff Dart has created some programs to help these individuals, but this jail is barely managing (Sullivan, L., January 20, 2014). "I can't conceive of anything more ridiculously stupid by government then to do what we're doing right now", (Sullivan, L., January 20, 2014). Instead of using "25 billion dollars a year maintaining federal buildings that are either unused or totally vacant" (Snyder, M. February 29, 2012), wouldn't it be more appropriate to build some of these buildings back up to be able to use them. I know of two specific places here in Michigan (and I am sure that there are more) that if they were fixed up they would be great for individuals that need help, but cannot receive the help. One instance is that there is no private lock down institutions for individuals with drug and alcohol issues in Michigan for individuals under the age of 18. The only way for individuals under the age of 18 to be able to get into a lock down facility in Michigan (which there are not very many) is to be in trouble with the law. What if someone wants help before they get in trouble with the law? This is another part of our government that is letting our children (our future) down.

There are times that individuals commit a crime (minor offense) just so they can get their medicine, because the local clinics closed down. The cost of annual spending for taxpayer's the courts being backed up do to cases like these is $10 million (Sullivan, L., January 20, 2014). Dart said that "he had no idea when he took the job of sheriff that he would also become the state's mental health provider" (Sullivan, L., January 20, 2014). As a society Americans try hard to take care of people that suffer with a sickness and basically show them sympathy. But, how many individuals show our mentally ill sympathy? Instead our mentally ill usually end up in handcuffs and are incarcerated (Sullivan, L., January 20, 2014). The way that our society acts is like making it a criminal offense to have a mental illness or to be diagnosed under the FASD umbrella. According to The New York Times these are a few data snapshots:

- Nationwide in America, more than three times as many mentally ill people are housed in prisons and jails as in hospitals, according to a 2010 study by the National Sheriffs' Association and Treatment Advocacy Center.
- Mentally ill inmates are often preyed upon while incarcerated, or disciplined because of trouble following rules. They are much more likely than other prisoners, for example, to be injured in a fight in jail, the Justice Department says.
- Some 40 percent of people with serious mental illnesses have been arrested at some point in their lives.

It seems to me that instead of moving forward in helping the mentally ill we are moving backwards. These individuals are not receiving the help that they need so instead of living in the community, like our government planned, these individuals are basically ending up in the same condition that our government was trying to get them out of, a locked up facility. Our government system has backfired and our government is not putting enough research into mental health to really help them. Instead our government would rather spend "30 million dollars on a program that was designed to help Pakistani farmers produce more mangos" (Snyder, M. February 29, 2012).

The American Psychological Association (APA) suggests three different types of screenings and evaluations to determine if an inmate is considered as having a mental illness. These are: 1) observation and structured inquiry,

2) intake mental health screening should take place within seven days of admission, and 3) the mental health evaluation is performed by a trained mental health professional (Metzner J.L. (1994). If an inmate is not evaluated for seven days what happens to them if they are on medication? There was a survey that was sent out to each state director of correctional mental health services in the United States and through these surveys 90% of the Department of Corrections (DOCs) stated that the screening for mental illness was "performed by either nurses or other health professionals" and "50% of the DOCs provided intake mental health screening for all recently arrived prisoners; 42% provided such screening to some recently arrived prisoner: and 8% of the DOCs did not provide intake mental health screenings (Metzner J.L. (1994). The purpose of performing mental health screenings and evaluations were first given for placing the inmate in the correct security level, however these screenings and evaluations are now utilized to see if an inmate needs mental health treatment.

In 2013 research suggested that individuals with mental illness were overrepresented in the criminal justice system, because of the lack of proper treatment that could have possibly prevented the incarceration of these mentally ill individuals (Horowitz, A., February 4, 2013). In the case of Armando Cruz he had been diagnosed with psychosis when he was 15 years old and later diagnosed with schizophrenia. In several cases when an inmate has a mental problem the individual is placed in solitary confinement, because the correctional officers do not know how to handle them and for the safety of themselves and others. However, solitary confinement for a mentally ill individual can be devastating for them. Like Armando Cruz that committed suicide while incarcerated and spent several years in solitary confinement (punishment for being mentally ill) (Metzner J.L. (1994). This is why I believe that more money needs to be put towards better and more accessible mental health programs that actually work.

MY FAMILY'S EXPERIENCE

Our family has been dealing with the mental health system for almost 18 years. The issues that are within our family are Major Clinical Depression, Dissociative Identity Disorder (DID, formerly called multiple personality), Mental Retardation, Cognitive Impairment, Fetal Alcohol Syndrome (FAS), Bi-Polar, ADHD, Oppositional Defiant Disorder, Psychosis, Schizophrenic, and Autism. Needless to say mental health professionals have been a big part of our lives. Although most of these professionals are very nice and understanding they need to follow policy, procedures, and laws. Most of the individuals that make these policy, procedures, and laws do not live with an individual that has mental disorders and they do not understand what these families go through. However, there was a push for more research on Autism because of a political figure. A mentally ill individual should not have to have a relative be a political figure to have more research completed on their particular disorder.

Several individuals are misdiagnosed and part of the reason is because the mental health professionals do not want to fully believe the parents/caregivers and in our case they did not want to believe the DID diagnosis that came from a forensic psychologist. Which in this case my daughter did not receive the proper treatment and part of the reason for that is because DID is such a controversial diagnosis every time that my daughter went into a mental hospital she would come out with a different diagnosis. When my daughter finally turned 18 they finally accepted the DID diagnosis. However with her cognitive impairment and mental retardation she does not completely understand the treatment. This is why there needs to be more research in the mental health field.

Being a parent of a child that has DID is very difficult. The longest job that I have been able to hold down was 7 years and that was when our daughter was young, once she hit the pre-teen years she started to become very hard to handle. It was hard for me to hold down a job, because I often received phone calls to either try to calm my daughter down over the phone or if it was real bad I needed to go home (which happened several times). Our daughter has between 10 and 12 different personalities and one of them (the male personality wants to kill me) and another personality wants to kill my wife. In order for us to feel safe to sleep at night we installed an alarm on our daughter's bedroom door and she used her school ID to bypass the alarm, so we ended up putting chairs in front of her bedroom door (she could get out, but we would hear her). What kind of life is that to live, to wonder if your daughter is going to kill you in the middle of the night?

We called the police several times on our daughter when she got out of control and I had to put her in a police hold until the police arrived. The police could see that I did not hurt her and I was protecting everybody in the house including my daughter from herself. She threatened suicide several times and attempted suicide three times. Two of the times that she attempted suicide she was in a mental hospital and the other time that she attempted suicide was in the organization that determines whether an individual needs to be hospitalized and when she did this they still sent her home. We had to lock up everything that was sharp in our home and there were several nights that we had to have friends and family members come over so that we could have a 24 hour watch on our daughter. How can CMH expect families to go through this, when they know that this is a lifetime disorder and no cure? I remember one time that we had to call an ambulance to take our daughter to the emergency room at our local hospital (CMH and ambulance policy) and the doctor saw our daughter going through the personality changes and the doctor just through his hands up in the air and told us that he had no idea how to handle a situation like this and told us that we would be better off handling her at this point.

This is not a way that a family should have to live. If more government spending was spent on research for mental health and having more beds for longer stays at the mental hospitals, maybe life would be easier for the individual that is mentally ill and the family members that love and take care of them. The first time that our daughter was in a mental hospital she was there for three months and when she came out there was a significant change for the better. Her hospital stays after that was shorter and there was not much of a change and the stays in the hospitals now are even getting shorter, the stays are now 3-10 days. How much help can these children that are severely mentally ill receive in that short of time?

When it comes to individuals that fall under the FASD umbrella it is a totally different story. My nephew (that my sister adopted) has FAS and as of right now there is not a treatment specifically for FAS. There are several other symptoms and diagnoses that go along with FAS and the two major ones are Bi-Polar and ADHD, which my nephew has and that is what his treatment is geared towards. However individuals that fall under the FASD umbrella have an addictive personality, so it is easy for them to become addicted to drugs/alcohol. Most of the time when these individuals felt that their medication has worked on the Bi-polar or ADHD they feel that they are cured and no longer need their medication, so they stop taking it. This most of the time leads to trouble with the legal system. These individuals go back on their medications until they feel they are well again and stop taking their medications and end up back in trouble with the law. This is another reason why more money needs to be spent on research here in the United States to help our own individuals first.

My nephew had overdosed 4 times, but he was not trying to kill himself he just liked the feeling of being high. He has been in therapy ever since I can remember, so would someone like to tell me where that therapy helped him, he will always feel the need to get high/drunk because of his FAS. He has just turned 18 and he has already been in trouble with the law and the way the police dealt with the whole situation was wrong, I was there and I witnessed the whole thing while it was going down. One of the first things that the officers did wrong was to question my nephew without him having representation. The police officers were told by both his mother and I that he has FAS, by law my nephew was not supposed to be able to waive his rights and be questioned without representation. The police were called because he hit his mother, but he was high and blacked out. He does not remember hitting his mother and he has told his therapists that he has blackouts, but nobody was dealing with these blackouts or giving him any advice on what to do when he feels that he is going to black out.

At one point my nephew was in the jail for juveniles. During his time there he was supposed to receive counseling/therapy, which he did. But it was for drug/alcohol abuse instead of the underlying problem of FAS. During my visits with him I have seen children as young as 10 years old in there. Also if Children's Village has too many problems with a child they will send them to a mental hospital. My question is why not try to get these children help in a mental hospital before sending them to the jail for juveniles, where they know that these children will not receive the appropriate help that they need.

My nephew is a very caring individual usually; his problems come from a birth defect called FAS. So instead of our country treating individuals that have FAS or some other mental illnesses our country treats them as criminals instead of victims. I am not saying that they should not have any consequences, but what I am saying is what good is putting an individual that has something wrong with them in jail. Most individuals that are mentally ill or are within the FASD umbrella have some cognitive impairment that is not easy to spot. Some of these individuals have normal IQ's but something inside their brain stops them from putting the consequences with the crime.

Right now my nephew is on probation and living in a three-quarter house and going to an alternative high school, but he had to get in trouble with the law before he could get any of this help. My question is why should an individual that has been born with a disability have to go through all of this and get a police record, because our mental health system is broken? Instead of cutting the funding for mental health maybe try cutting some government workers salaries. Our country is in trouble and not taking care of our youth that will be running our country one day, what will our country turn into? I am proud to be an American, but I am discouraged in the way that our government is taking care of our country. We as taxpayers are paying the salaries of the individuals that are ruining our country. Remember take care of our children, so that our future can be taken care of.

REFERENCES

Adubato, S., & Cohen, D. (2011). Diagnosis, Assessment and New Directions in Research and Multimodal Treatment. *Prenatal Alcohol Use and FASD,* 3-29. doi:978-1-60805-031-4

Frederick, J.M. (October 24, 1999). *Michigan Department of Family Independence Agency.* retrieved 10/4/2015, from http:/falseallegations.com/michigan.htm

Horowitz, A. (February 4, 2013). *Mental Illness Soars In Prisons, Jails While Inmates Suffer.* retrieved 9/13/2015, from Mental Illness Soars In Prisons, Jails While Inmates Suffer Web Site: http://www.huffingtonpost.com2013/02/04/mental-illness-prisons-jails-inmates_n_26100.

Mental Health and the Role of the States. (June 2015). *The Pew Charitable Trusts and the John D. and Catherine T. MacArthur Foundation .* Retrieved 10/16/2015, from http://www.pewtrusts.org/~/media/assets/2015/06/mentalhealthandroleofstatesreport.pdf?la=en

K & C Michigan Abuse and Neglect Defense Attorneys. (n.d) retrieved 10/4/2015, from Michigan Spanking Law and Facts Is Spanking Legal?

Web Site: http://abuseandneglectdefense.com/ michigan-spanking-law-and-facts/

Kellerman, T. (n.d.). *Fact Sheet for Personnel in Law Enforcement.* retrieved 10/16/2015, from Fetal Alcohol Syndrome Disorders Web Site: http://come-over.to/FAS/ LawEnforcement.htm

Knakal, R. (October 1, 2013). Here's a List of Stupid Things the Government Spends Money On. *Commercial Observer.* Web Site: htt://commercialobserver.com/2013/10/ heres-a-list-of-stupid-things-the-government-spe...

Kristof, N. (02/08/2014). Inside a Mental Hospital Called Jail. *The New York Times Sunday Review.* Web Site: http://www.nytimes.com/2014/02/09/opinion/sunday/ inside-a-mental-...

Lewis, R. (April 8, 2014). *US prisons home to 10 times as many mentally ill as in state hospitals.* retrieved 9/13/2015, from http//america.aljazeera.com/articles/2014/4/8mental-illness-prison.html

Metzner J.L. (1994). Mental Health Screening and Evaluation Within Prisons. *Bull Am Acad Psychiatry Law. 22*, 3.

Mince-Didier, A. (n.d.) *Criminal Consequences of Spanking Your Children.* (n.d) retrieved 10/4/2015, from Criminal Consequences of Spanking Your Children/Criminal Law Web Site: http://www.criminaldefenselawyer.com/resources/ criminal-defense/cr...

(n.d) retrieved October 1, 2015, from State Budget Office Web Site: http://www.michigan.gov/budget/0,4538,7-40794-139075--F,00.html

Ranking America. (n.d) retrieved October 2, 2015, from http://rankingamerica.wordpress.com/category/education/page/3/

Snyder, M. (February 29, 2012). *30 Stupid Things The Government Is Spending Money.* retrieved September 11, 2015, from http://endoftheamericandream.com/archives/30-stupid-things-the-governemnt-is-spendin...

Substance Abuse and Mental Health Services Administration. *Addressing Fetal Alcohol Spectrum Disorders (FASD.* Treatment Improvement Protocol (TIP) Series 58. HHS Publication No. (SMA) 13-4803. Rockville, MD: Substance Abuse and Mental Health Services Administration, 2014.

Sullivan, L (January 20, 2014). *Mentally Ill Are Often Locked Up In Jails That Can't Help.* retrieved September 13, 2015, from npr Web Site: http://www.npr.org/2014/01/20/263461940/mentally-ill-inmates-often-...

Wilde, M. (n.d.) *Global grade: How do U.S. students compare?.* (n.d) retrieved October 2, 2015, from http://www.greatschools.org/gk/articles/u-s-students-compare/